BOURNEMOUTH owes its existence to a woman's wish to swim. It was 1810 and Henrietta Tregonwell and her husband Lewis, a Yeomanry, were visiting what was then a secluded coastal valley, cut by the tiny Bourne Stream. 'Sea-bathing' was newly fashionable, and the beach at Bournemouth – as it was called – waves lapped at a sandy beach that stretched to either horizon. Summer's warmth brought out the scent of pine trees. Inland lay only heather and heath. Henrietta Tregonwell thought it paradise, and persuaded her husband to build a house overlooking the sea in which to spend part of the summer. Miraculously, that house still survives, though encased in what is now the Royal Exeter Hotel.

Prior to the arrival of the Tregonwells a few smallholders scratched a meagre living from the area's poor sandy soil. Only the smuggling gangs prospered; their lines of pack-ponies heading across the heath laden with wine, spirits and tea illegally landed on the beaches. In 1805, the year of Trafalgar, 5000 acres of the heath were enclosed and sold, mostly to local gentry. It was some of this land that the Tregonwells had bought, and on which, in due course, they built a few seaside cottages for friends to rent.

The statue of Bournemouth's founder, Lewis Tregonwell, outside the Bournemouth International Centre. He is holding a scroll with the names of the three Bournemouth men to have won the Victoria Cross.

Speculators and local landowners soon followed their example. Within 30 years the first roads had been laid-out, the Bath Hotel and a boarding house had opened their doors, and a cluster of large marine villas overlooked the Bourne Stream on land sloping down to the sea. The scrub either side of the stream was transformed into a pleasure garden, complete with rustic bridges and a charge for admission. Today, as the Lower Gardens, they are free to all and together with the Central and Upper Gardens remain perhaps the town's most popular feature.

As well as the sea and pine trees, of which 3 million were planted during Victorian times, Bournemouth's principal attraction was its mild winter climate, which made it, to quote a French guide book, 'a most suitable residence for delicate constitutions.' The town's first residents were convalescents and the well-to-do, their comforts maintained

Bournemouth's heart is the pedestrianised Square, seen here looking west towards Commercial Road with one of the town's familiar yellow buses in the foreground. In 1810 Bournemouth consisted of a wayside inn on the lonely track between Poole and Christchurch. The Bourne Stream was crossed by a plank bridge where the Square is today. Nearby stood a cottage, with beehives, a small garden and some meadowland carved out of the surrounding heath.

The old photograph shows the same view in about 1900.

The Town Centre

Above A second view of the Square, looking over the circular roof of the Obscura café towards the foot of Richmond Hill and Old Christchurch Road.

Below Guest houses in Upper Terrace Road. Despite the jokes about landladies, the town's guest houses and Bed & Breakfast establishments have played an important role in its history, offering friendly family-run accommodation since the opening of the railway in 1870. As holiday habits have changed, many have closed their doors. In the 1930s there were 2,500 guest houses, of which less than 80 remain open.

by a small army of servants. By 1850 Bournemouth's population was about 1,000 and it was beginning to acquire the trappings of a town. Daily stagecoaches rumbled across the heath to Christchurch and Southampton. Bathing machines lined the beach, which by 1855 boasted a short wooden pier. The Tregonwell Arms doubled as the post office. There was a volunteer fire brigade, a dispensary and school. Until the opening of St Peter's Church in 1845, the town's sole place of worship was in a pair of converted cottages beside a decoy pond for wildfowling, near where the Square is today.

By 1860 the population had risen to

Above Christmas decorations add seasonal colour to the shops in the Arcade, the covered link between Old Christchurch Road and Gervis Place which first opened in 1866.

Right Shoppers in Old Christchurch Road. On the right are the town's two oldest department stores, Dingles and Beales. Dingles began life as Bright's Stores, and was opened by a former missionary recently returned from India in 1875, whilst Beales owes its success to a hard-working son of a Weymouth ship's captain called John Elmes Beales, who in 1881 invested every penny he could scrape together in a drapery called the Fancy Fair in St Peter's Terrace. By the 1930s, much enlarged and with eight rows of lifts serving seven floors, it was *the* fashionable shop in Bournemouth. Despite being badly bombed in the war, Beales remains in the control of the family and enjoys the loyalty of generations of Bournemouth shoppers.

1,701. By 1880 it was over 16,000, and by end of the century it nudged 70,000. A key factor in Bournemouth's meteoric growth was the arrival of the railway in 1870. For years the townspeople argued against its coming lest it encourage working-class 'trippers' and pubs to open on Sundays. Financial commonsense inevitably triumphed over middle-class gentility. On August Bank Holiday weekends literally thousands of holidaymakers stepped down onto the station platforms, laden with buckets and spades and determined to enjoy themselves, leading in turn to the opening of the many family-run guest houses that have helped give Bournemouth its character. As the town expanded, the need for bricklayers, plumbers, plasterers and joiners led to the first satellite suburbs spilling out across the heath – at first in isolated and seemingly random terraces, and finally in lines of nearly identical streets which filled the green spaces in between with brick, stucco and pebbledash housing.

Despite the holidaymakers and trams, the shopping arcades and commerce; despite

Left The War Memorial in the Central Gardens, with the Town Hall in the background. The Town Hall began life as the Mont Dore Hotel, and was bought by the Council shortly after the First World War. The War Memorial commemorates the 650 men of Bournemouth who died in that war, as well as those who lost their lives in the Second World War.

Below left The richly decorated interior of Bournemouth's first parish church, St Peter's. The original building opened in 1845, but the church that greets worshippers today is the slightly later work of the architect G.E. Street (also responsible for London's Law Courts and four other Bournemouth churches). The church's interior has been described as a 'jewel box', and with its stained glass and wealth of colour and ornamentation is rightly regarded as one of the most beautiful of all Victorian churches. Outside are memorial stones to Bournemouth men killed in the Second World War and buried abroad, whilst on the bank overlooking the church is a tomb to the feminist Mary Wollstonecraft (died 1797), her daughter Mary Shelley (died 1851) and author of *Frankenstein*, and the heart of Mary's husband, the poet Shelley, who drowned off Italy in 1822. Shelley's washed-up corpse was burnt on the beach by some friends, one of whom plucked his heart from the flames.

Below Local artists exhibit and sell their work from stalls in Pine Walk during the annual Summer Art Exhibition in the Lower Gardens.

Above The Royal Bath Hotel in Bath Road has long been one of Bournemouth's most celebrated hotels. It opened as the Bath Hotel in 1838, acquiring the 'Royal' after being bought in 1876 by Sir Merton Russell-Cotes, who added two wings and used it to display his art collection. Its guests have included princes, prime ministers and rock stars, but the most unlikely are the men of the Royal Canadian Air Force, billeted in it for much of the Second World War. Today it has 140 bedrooms, two restaurants, an indoor swimming pool, gymnasium, conference rooms and banqueting suites.

Right A yellow bus passes the Royal Exeter Hotel, Exeter Road. The hotel incorporates Bournemouth's first private house, the summer retreat built by Lewis Tregonwell and his wife Henrietta in 1811. Ten years earlier, when Napoleon threatened to invade, Tregonwell had been a captain in the Dorset Yeomanry, and it was to show his second wife the area of coast under his command that first brought them on a visit to Bourne Mouth.

Edward VII when Prince of Wales installing his mistress Lillie Langtry in the town, Victorian Bournemouth never shook off its air of well-heeled respectability – indeed, some would argue it never has! Nannies pushed prams through the pines, or along the newly laid out promenade of Undercliff Drive, whilst their employers sipped tea and listened to afternoon concerts amidst the potted plants that filled the soaring glass and wrought iron of the now demolished Winter Gardens. Also demolished is the house near Alum Chine where Robert Louis Stevenson wrote *Kidnapped*, as is the bridge in the chine from where Winston Churchill fell 29 feet as a boy, and whose descent, if not halted by the branches of

Above Two views of the Russell-Cotes Art Gallery & Museum, which overlooks the East Cliff Promenade and Poole Bay. Sir Merton Russell-Cotes (1835-1921) was the son of a Midlands ironmaster who moved to Bournemouth in 1876 and quickly shook-up the staid Victorian town. He bought and enlarged the Royal Bath Hotel, filling it with his vast collection of paintings and objects. In 1894 he built what is now the museum as a birthday present for his wife Annie, and once completed they gave the Italian-style seaside villa and its contents to the town, on condition that they be allowed to live in it for their lifetimes. It opened as a museum in 1919, and is particularly noted for its collections of Japanese art, silver, ceramics and contemporary crafts. The foreground sculpture is by Tim Harrisson.

Below Cutting-edge architecture, the Central Library at the Triangle. The £10 million horseshoe-shaped building, which includes a café and some shopping space, opened in 2002 and went on to win the Prime Minister's Better Building Award.

a pine tree, might have changed the course of our nation's history.

By the dawn of the twentieth century Bournemouth was bustling and prosperous. Shops filled with the latest fashions lined Westover and Old Christchurch Roads. In summer, excursion paddle steamers berthed alongside the new pier – whose seaward end included a bandstand. By now neighbouring Boscombe also boasted a pier, which together with its hotels, marine villas and shop-lined Royal Arcade were proof of its transformation from gorse-covered common. Such changes were typical of the suburbs that ringed central Bournemouth. Professional people built large villas in Westbourne, whilst what a contemporary report described as the 'labouring and industrial classes' settled in Winton and Moordown. An attempt to turn Southbourne into a resort rivalling Bournemouth fell victim to winter storms. Kinson remained a village. Pokesdown developed round its railway station. Charminster lay the far side of Queens Park.

Wallisdown was an isolated scatter of houses circled by heath, Talbot Village still farmland and model cottages.

The period between the two World Wars confirmed Bournemouth's reputation as a south coast resort. Special trains like the 'Pines Express' linked it to the Midlands, bringing yet more holidaymakers, who were ferried to and fro by the town's fleet of double-decker trams and green and red buses. After a day on the sands, the children fed and put to bed, their parents flocked to the Pavilion, which opened in 1929 and as well as a theatre and ballroom included restaurants and bars.

The outbreak of war ten years later brought the holiday trains to a halt. Visitors were banned, hotels requisitioned for military use. The sandcastles were replaced by barbed wire and anti-invasion defences. The worst raid of the war came at a Sunday lunchtime in May 1943 when an enemy bomber dropped 40 bombs on the town, killing 208 men and women.

Above The Pavilion has been a feature of the Lower Gardens since it opened in 1929. Incorporating a concert hall, restaurants and ballroom, it stands on the site of the Belle Vue Hotel. The restoration of the Pavilion is to be part of a £59 million town centre development project, which will include rooftop gardens, restaurants and a casino.

Below The fountain outside the Pavilion, with Westover Road in the background.

Opposite page One of the landmarks of modern Bournemouth is the 'Eye', which rises to 500 feet from its base in the Lower Gardens.

Above The view from the Bournemouth 'Eye'. The basket can take up to 30 passengers, and provides panoramic views out over the town and Poole Bay.

Right Summer in the Square. Bournemouth's centre is increasingly pedestrian friendly, adding greatly to its enjoyment and – in fine weather – a European sense of café culture.

After D-Day the wartime restrictions were relaxed, and not a summer weekend has gone by since when blue skies and warm sun haven't seen Bournemouth's beaches packed from end to end.

The beaches are only part of the reason for Bournemouth's enduring popularity. A stroll through the Central Gardens takes you to shopping streets the equal of any along the south coast. The opening of the Bournemouth International Centre has provided a venue for conferences and stars from the world of entertainment. Improved transport links have brought employment as well as visitors, and a population now nudging 175,000. New routes to Europe are annually being opened from Bournemouth International Airport. Despite the perception that the area is full of retired people, the 17,000 students at Bournemouth University and the many more who attend the language schools for which the town is now known have kept it moving forward and willing to embrace the new. As befits a town barely two centuries old, Bournemouth remains young at heart.

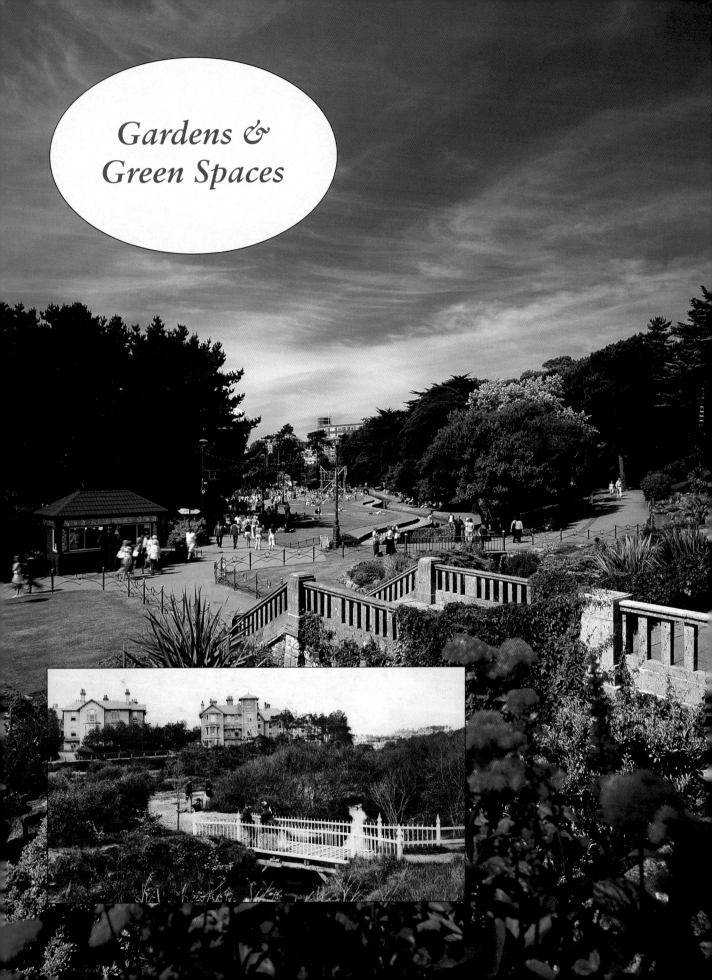

Gardens &
Green Spaces

Opposite page The Lower Gardens. On the right is the Pine Walk, known as the Invalids' Walk until 1916 when the council decided a change of name might improve Bournemouth's image. No such changes have been necessary for the three main town centre gardens, which together with the beaches are surely the brightest jewels in Bournemouth's crown. The Lower Gardens once belonged to the Tapps-Gervis-Meyrick family, and it was their architect, Decimus Burton (designer of the Arch at Hyde Park Corner) who suggested that ten acres of scrub and pine trees either side of the Bourne Stream should be laid out as pleasure gardens. They became town property in 1873, when new walks and plantations were laid out. There have been improvements and new plantings to all three principal gardens, but their original design and character have largely been retained.

The old photograph shows the Lower Gardens in 1865. The building on the right is now the Hermitage Hotel in Exeter Road and the rustic wooden bridge is roughly where the stone bridge in the modern photograph is today.

Above Listening to the band in the Lower Gardens.

Below 'Bournemouth in Bloom' in the Lower Gardens. The Lower Gardens are renowned for their floral bedding displays and the coloured foliage plants used to create the town's motto and crest.

Above Coy Pond is at the head of the Upper Gardens. Although it takes its name from an old decoy pond for wildfowling it was actually dug out in the 1880s to provide soil for the nearby railway.

Left Spring in the Upper Gardens. The fake medieval tower was built as a water tower in 1885 to power the sprinklers for the gardens.

Below The tennis courts in the Central Gardens.

The boggy Bourne Stream is now a neat channel running through the heart of the Central Gardens. Both the Upper and Central Gardens were once rough grazing belonging to the Durrant family. In 1871 they were acquired by the town, thus creating a two mile garden stretching up the Bourne Valley from the seafront to Coy Pond.

Autumn colour in the Central Gardens. The path is part of the Bourne Valley Greenway, an inspired 2004 development which forms a continuous car-free track for 4 miles from the seafront to Canford Heath. As far as Coy Pond it is wheelchair friendly, beyond which it crosses Talbot Heath and Bourne Bottom. Anyone interested in what the area once looked like should walk as far as Talbot Heath and see this last reminder of the barren uncultivated heath on which Bournemouth and its satellite townships are built.

Above The five acres of Seafield Gardens provide a green space for recreation in the middle of Southbourne. The bowls green and pavilion are nearly 100 years old, and there is also a croquet lawn, tennis courts, and a children's play area. The wonderfully over-the-top water tower was originally built in 1898, and is now a privately owned Listed building.

Below left A centrepiece of Boscombe Chine Gardens is this old train engine covered with bedding plants.

Below right Putting for the pin at the Queen's Park Golf Course. Bournemouth's green spaces owe much to the foresight of its founding fathers, and the generosity of its principal landowners. Wessex Way now divides the 173 acres of Queen's Park from the smaller 86 acre King's Park, but both were laid out on rough grazing land originally belonging to Sir George Meyrick, whose name lives on in a third park on land he donated to the town. Golfers have walked the Queen's Park fairways since the course opened in 1905.

Palm and pine in the Tropical Gardens at the
seaward end of Alum Chine. The chine takes its name from
the alum mined nearby in the 16th century, when alum was used in
tanning and dyeing. The terraced Tropical Gardens were laid out with
paths and drystone walls in the 1920s and still include a handful of
eighty-year-old Chusan Palms from the original planting.

Bournemouth Pier and the beach from West Cliff. The town owes its popularity to seven miles of sand, stretching from Branksome Dene Chine to Hengistbury Head. Despite the groynes spaced the length of the beach, tidal drift and winter storms are constantly moving the sand east, and much of it has to be regularly brought back from off the Isle of Wight: most recently 1.5 million cubic metres was dredged from the seabed and returned to Bournemouth. The Dorset Belle pleasure boats leaving the pier operate daily cruises throughout the season, as well as special sunset and firework cruises. The Needles at the western end of the Isle of Wight are visible in the background.

The Beaches

Right West Beach from the pier. To the left is the clifftop Marriott Highcliff Hotel, which opened in 1873 and is popular with prime ministers during the conference season. The brick-built Bournemouth International Centre (opened 1984), or BIC, dominates the centre of the photograph. As well as conferences, it attracts some of the biggest names in entertainment. A garage and four Victorian hotels were demolished to make way for it – a lucky survivor is the Court Royal Hotel, seen here squeezed behind the Oceanarium.

Below A high speed ride on *Shockwave* is fifteen minutes of pure adrenalin. The 880 horse-power Jet Drive engine can take the boat's speed up to 30 knots, and it can literally spin through 360° in its own length.

Opposite page Sunset over the beaches.

Below A lifeguard on the beach. The town's beaches are patrolled throughout the summer by the Bournemouth Lifeguard Corps and RNLI Beach Lifeguards.

Left Blue skies and surf. Bournemouth's beaches regularly receive Blue Flag Awards, which are based on such things as water quality, safety, and environmental concerns.

Opposite page Catching the last waves. Plans are moving forward to build a £1.5 million artificial reef about 500 yards off Boscombe, thus creating consistent waves up to 6 feet high during the winter and dramatically improving the surfing.

Below A heatwave in the summer school holidays can barely leave room for a towel on Bournemouth's beaches, and it is estimated that up to 15,000 people flock on to the sand in warm weather, many of whom are enjoying the sunshine in this view looking east towards Boscombe. The East Cliff Lift is visible beyond the children's slide. The electrically-powered East and West Cliff Lifts are both a hundred years old, whilst the town's third cliff lift, at Fisherman's Walk, dates to 1935. The building with the red pinnacles on top of the cliff is the Russell-Cotes Art Gallery & Museum, whilst to its left is the Royal Bath Hotel. Behind them lies the increasingly higher Bournemouth skyline, much of it blocks of apartments.

Above Looking east across Poole Bay from the garden of the Russell-Cotes Museum & Art Gallery. The 858 feet long pier is the town's third, and was opened in 1880. During the Second World War the middle section was demolished to stop it being used by an invading enemy. The Pier Theatre is home to summer shows and light entertainment.

Left The paddle steamer *Waverley* alongside Bournemouth Pier. Compare this photograph with the old photograph below, which shows the pier as it was in 1872 after a gale had destroyed the pierhead. Nearly a century and a half may separate the two photographs, yet both include a paddle steamer: the *Heather Belle* shown leaving for Swanage in the old photograph provided the first regular steamer service, often with a band playing on deck. By 1900 there was the occasional £1 excursion to Cherbourg. *Waverley* is the world's last sea-going paddle steamer and is a regular summer visitor to Bournemouth.

Fireworks fired simultaneously at both Bournemouth and Boscombe piers light up the night sky, watched by boats in the bay and the spectators lining the West Undercliff Promenade.

The line of brightly-coloured 1930s beach huts on West Beach are just some of Bournemouth's 1500 beach huts and 572 seafront chalets. In Victorian times, men and women bathed on separate beaches, changing in bathing machines which were then towed out to sea by horses. Even as late as the 1920s changing in public was frowned on. The beach hut was the solution – a place to put granny and the budgerigar, boil a kettle, or take shelter from the British weather. Those in Bournemouth can be rented for a week or day, though there is often a waiting list.

Opposite page Looking east towards Southbourne, with Bournemouth beyond, from near Hengistbury Head. The headland marks the first break in a built-up area that stretches west all the way to the entrance to Poole Harbour, 10 miles away.

Left The Royal Arcade, Boscombe. Boscombe's growth was slow, and much of the initial development was by its principal landowners, Sir Percy Shelley and Sir Henry Wolff. Gradually plots were sold and laid out for housing or marine villas. The opening of the pier in 1889 was followed a few years later by the building of the Royal Arcade, Salisbury Hotel and Hippodrome Theatre by Archibald Beckett in an attempt to rival the centre of Bournemouth. Beckett founded the Boscombe Band to put on daily concerts in the arcade, which had seats down the centre, and there were organ recitals there until quite recently.

Below left The other Victorian arcade is at Westbourne, which was built in 1884 by Henry Joy, who also built the Bournemouth Arcade, and whose name is inscribed high up on the inside above the entrances. The tiled paving was once a different pattern for every shop.

Below Seamoor Road, Westbourne. The half moon of Seamoor Road and the wide range of shops lining Poole Road make Westbourne seem compact. Only a mile from Alum Chine and the beaches, still well-wooded and largely residential, it retains the atmosphere of a prosperous village. To its immediate west is 'County Gates', where Poole begins and which until Bournemouth became part of Dorset in 1972 marked the Hampshire/ Dorset boundary.

Out & About

Above Corn has been ground at Throop Mill since Saxon times, for a mill on the site is certainly mentioned in the Domesday Book. The present building dates to the turn of the 20th century, when new machinery was installed. The now disused mill is occasionally open, and there is a good walk along the River Stour that passes beside it.

Below The Hawk aircraft of the Royal Air Force Aerobatic Team, the Red Arrows, lined up for refuelling on the runway at Bournemouth International Airport before performing their annual summer display over Bournemouth seafront.

Below right St Andrew's Church, Millhams Lane, Kinson. At the start of the 19th century, when Bournemouth was uninhabited, Kinson was a thriving farming village of 500. A churchyard gravestone records a smuggler called Robert Trotman, 'murdered' in 1795, and the lovely Norman tower has grooves worn in the heathstone by ropes hauling up barrels of smuggled brandy.

Above Iford Bridge marks the first medieval crossing over the River Stour upstream from Christchurch. The original bridge has long vanished, and the present bridge is in three sections, of which one is for flood relief. The main channel is bridged by four stone arches. Today the busy A35 crosses the Stour by a bridge built in 1933 (just visible in the background), and the 13 feet wide carriageway of the old bridge is limited to pedestrians.

Right The River Stour at Tuckton Bridge. The first bridge here opened in 1883 as a wooden toll bridge, which Bournemouth Council bought twenty years later to enable them to extend their tram routes right through to Christchurch. After taking down the old bridge, they replaced it with what at the time was one of the first reinforced concrete bridges in the country, and which today marks the end of the navigable river for all but small motorboats.

Below Flowering cherries and spring tulips at Tuckton, with the River Stour in the background.

Above The Littledown Centre sits within 47 acres of park opposite The Royal Bournemouth Hospital on Castle Lane East. It opened in 1989, and its facilities include swimming pools, a spa, sports hall, gym, café and bar, as well as a cricket pitch, artificial football pitches and a miniature railway.

Above The Almshouses, Talbot Village. In 1835 Georgina and Mary Anne Talbot, the two unmarried daughters of Sir George Talbot, bought 465 acres of heath with the intention of creating a model village. When finished in the 1860s it comprised six farms, a church, school, almshouses and 19 cottages – some of which can be seen opposite the University on Wallisdown Road. Each cottage was provided with an acre of garden, and though the farms had grazing rights over the heath they were only allowed to sell eggs, bacon, poultry and homemade jam. The largest of the farms, Talbot Village Farm, is now the site of Bournemouth University.

Below Talbot Campus, Bournemouth University. The University was established in 1992 and today has over 17,000 students at its two principal campuses, Talbot and Lansdowne. It has traditionally focused on professional vocational courses, such as nursing, and has a celebrated Media School. In the foreground is the Geological Terrace, 170 hand-cut stone blocks arranged in geological age order.

Late afternoon sunlight on the tower of Christchurch Priory, from near the junction of the rivers Stour and Avon. The town sits between the two rivers, and a visit makes a good day out from Bournemouth, if only for the priory, which dates almost completely from shortly after the Norman Conquest to the time of Henry VIII. There are some fine memorials, including one to the poet Shelley, whose heart is buried at St Peter's, Bournemouth.

The view east from the heath of Hengistbury Head towards Christchurch Harbour and Mudeford Spit.

Left Mudeford Spit and the entrance to Christchurch Harbour. The Spit is famous for its beach huts, which are double banked, with some facing out to sea, others towards the Harbour.

Below Hengistbury Head. Walking on the windswept heathland on a winter's day it is hard to believe that nearly 500,000 people live within a short car journey. As well as being a Nature Reserve, it is one of the most historically important places in Britain, combining Stone Age sites dating back nearly 15,000 years and Bronze Age barrows that have yielded gold-covered buttons and an amber necklace. One reminder of its past are the massive earth bank fortifications of the Double Dyke, which cuts across the entire headland near the main car park. They were built in the Iron Age to protect what was then a busy port trading with Rome and continental Europe – and when Bournemouth did not exist.